Okay, Spanner, Yo...

DAVID CLAYTON

Illustrated by Trevor Parkin

OXFORD

UNIVERSITY PRESS

Great Clarendon Street, Oxford OX2 6DP

Oxford University Press is a department of the University of Oxford.
It furthers the University's objective of excellence in research, scholarship,
and education by publishing worldwide in

Oxford   New York

Auckland Cape Town Dar es Salaam Hong Kong Karachi
Kuala Lumpur Madrid Melbourne Mexico City Nairobi
New Delhi Shanghai Taipei Toronto

With offices in

Argentina Austria Brazil Chile Czech Republic France Greece
Guatemala Hungary Italy Japan Poland Portugal Singapore
South Korea Switzerland Thailand Turkey Ukraine Vietnam

Oxford is a registered trade mark of Oxford University Press
in the UK and in certain other countries

Text © David Clayton 1999

The moral rights of the author have been asserted

Database right Oxford University Press (maker)

First published 1996
This edition 2005

All rights reserved. No part of this publication may be reproduced,
stored in a retrieval system, or transmitted, in any form or by any means,
without the prior permission in writing of Oxford University Press,
or as expressly permitted by law, or under terms agreed with the appropriate
reprographics rights organization. Enquiries concerning reproduction
outside the scope of the above should be sent to the Rights Department,
Oxford University Press, at the address above

You must not circulate this book in any other binding or cover
and you must impose this same condition on any acquirer

British Library Cataloguing in Publication Data
Data available

ISBN: 978-0-19-918410-1

15 17 19 20 18 16 14

Available in packs
Stage 14 Pack of 6:
ISBN: 978-0-19-918406-4
Stage 14 Class Pack:
ISBN: 978-0-19-918413-2
Guided Reading Cards also available:
ISBN: 978-0-19-918415-6

Cover artwork by Trevor Parkin

Printed in Malaysia by
MunSang Printers Sdn Bhd

Paper used in the production of this book is a natural, recyclable product
made from wood grown in sustainable forests. The manufacturing process
conforms to the environmental regulations of the country of origin.

CHAPTER 1

We want our medals

'Tonight's the night!' Spanner Cavanagh peered through his wire glasses at the rainy bus window.

'Yes,' said Del, staring into the darkness.

'Good job your dad fixed up for us to play indoors on the City Dome astro. We could never play outside in this,' said Porky.

'No,' said Del.

'How many are you going to score tonight, Del?' Senna was bouncing up and down on his seat too.

'Dunno.'

'Last time we played them you got six!'

'Four,' said Del.

'Well, anyway, we'll walk it with you playing!'

The whole team was wild with excitement, especially Spanner. He was the third reserve and was only on the team because his mother washed the team's shirts. But Clogger and Simmo both had 'flu and this was his big chance.

'STEELHOUSE – STEELHOUSE!
STEELHOUSE – STEELHOUSE!
WE'LL SUPPORT YOU EVER MORE...'

'Quiet, back there!' said the driver and Spanner stopped singing.

Del sat silent. Soon it was his stop.
'See you at seven, Del!' yelled Senna as Del got up.

'Yeah,' shouted Spanner. 'Don't go missing. WE WANT OUR MEDALS!'

Del watched the flickering bus lights slip away into the gloom. Spanner's words echoed in his head.

We want our medals. Is that me, he thought – MR MEDALS?

There were other things he liked to do: playing on his keyboard and his computer and just messing about. Life wasn't only football.

But football had taken him over.

There was the school team in midweek, City Juniors on Saturdays and Steelhouse Blues on Sundays.

And then there was Dad.

Rod Taylor was ex-England, ex-United, but he was still good – he now played for City.

And there was Harry Green, running City Juniors on Saturdays and Steelhouse on Sundays.

How many games had Del played since he was seven? How many goals had he scored? Dad knew.

He had played two hundred and seven games and scored nine hundred and ninety-seven goals. Dad wrote it all down in a book.

'That lad's a genius! Better than his dad,' Harry Green had said, again and again.

Del was sick of hearing it. He wasn't sick of football. He wasn't sick of the lovely swish as the ball hit the net. Just sick of the pressure and shouting and questions. Tired of Harry Green screeching and roaring even though Steelhouse never lost.

CHAPTER 2

'Come on, Del!'

An hour after Del arrived home, his dad was already looking at his watch.

'All set?' said his dad.

'Okay.'

'What's the matter? Aren't you feeling well?'

'I'm okay, Dad.'

'Is it nerves?'

I just want to be left alone, thought Del. But he said, 'I'm okay.'

'Well, I hope so. It's a big night tonight.'

'I know.'

'A lot of important people will be watching you.'

'I know.'

'Aren't you interested?'

Dad's voice had that edge again. Things had not gone so well recently for City. The senior team had been losing and now Del could tell his dad wasn't pleased with him. The footballer's green eyes were shining with irritation.

'Yes, Dad, but…' He started to explain what he was feeling, but his dad wasn't listening.

'I don't understand you. When I was your age…' Del closed his eyes. Dad's voice played the same record again and again.

Steelhouse hadn't lost for three years. He had already scored hundreds of goals. What more did Dad want?

'Yes, Dad.'

'... I'd have given anything to be as good as you...'

'Yes, Dad.'

'It took me years, years...'

'Yes, Dad.'

'Loads of kids would give their right arm to be as good as you...'

'Sorry, Dad.' Del felt guilty, just the way he did when his gran told him about all those starving children in Africa when he didn't finish his lunch.

The phone rang to save him.

'Del, it's for you – Spanner,' Mum called.

Good old Spanner! Getting him off the hook!

'Are you ready?' shouted Spanner. 'I am. I'm so excited... And Mum's washed the shirts TWICE!'

'Wonderful,' said Del. 'We'll be the cleanest team in the league.'

'Ha! That's a good one!' Spanner laughed. 'See you at seven.'

Del put the phone down.

His dad cut in quickly. 'And another thing...'

BEEP – BEEP!

Del picked the phone up again.

'Del? Harry here. You still all right for tonight?'

'Yes, Harry,' sighed Del. 'I'm all right.'

He put the phone down.

'As I was saying...' Dad tried again.

BEEP – BEEP!

This time it was Senna, the goalie.

Del put the phone down again. It's only football! he thought. They've all gone mad.

Soon it was time to go. He slipped upstairs for his bag. The medals hanging on the wall reminded him of what Spanner had said on the bus. *We want our medals.* He stood staring at them.

But not for long. His Dad's voice came up the stairs. 'Come on, Del! I'm waiting.'

It wasn't far to the stadium, twenty minutes in his dad's car. Dad drove without speaking. Del was glad. His mind was a jumble of mixed-up thoughts.

Who am I doing this for? Me? The lads? Dad? This is mad! I should be loving it. Everybody thinks I do. And I do – sometimes.

'Here now.' His dad's sharp voice popped the bubble of his thoughts.

Up ahead of them were the great concrete hills of the stands with the silent, steel giraffes of the floodlights watching over them. The giant indoor sports complex was round the back.

As soon as they saw Del, everyone wanted to talk to him.

Harry Green was boasting again. 'We'll hammer them. Just give it to Del and we'll walk it!' The coach had run Steelhouse for twenty years and he had never had a great team before. Then Del Taylor changed all that.

Spanner ran up. 'I'm dreaming!' he said, grinning from ear to ear. 'I'm in a CUP FINAL at City's ground!'

Del and Spanner had been friends ever since they were little. It was hard not to like Spanner. He was so keen.

Secretly, Del wondered why Spanner liked playing football so much. He was hopeless. He had never even scored in a proper match!

The two boys were very different. Del had always been quiet. He was a bit of a loner. Spanner was always joking. He was so good tempered that he put everyone in a good mood. But tonight, Del found it hard to grin, even at his friend.

Del just sat staring. He knew what he could do. Trouble was, he didn't want to do it any more. He felt more alone than he had ever done in his life.

CHAPTER 3

'Leave me alone'

The others were used to Del sitting by himself. Del always concentrated, always sat quietly before a match. The quiet before the storm of goals. They'd never seen anyone like Del.

But when Del sat alone this time it was different. He had made up his mind. This was going to be his last game. But how would he tell everyone? How would he tell Dad? That was the problem.

Everyone else was excited. Spanner went to the toilet five times. The other players grinned. They could see their medals in front of them already.

Soon it was time for Steelhouse to run on to the pitch, collars up, with Del leading the way.

Vernon Park crept on, goggling at the great glass-domed roof and massive emerald pitch.

Then they eyed Del. He was juggling the ball, flicking it right over his head, then back-heeling it over to halt, once again, on his foot. They remembered the four goals from last time.

Del looked up and saw his dad wave from the gallery bar. It was packed out with scouts looking for new talent. His dad must have told them to come.

And so the Stockdale Under-12s Cup Final began. You could tell the game had started, not only because the ref had blown, but because Harry Green had started his dance on the touchline.

'Hit it! Hold it! Push it! LEAVE IT! For heaven's sake!'

He ranted like a mad parrot. His favourite screech was 'Give it to Del!'

But Del made sure that he was running the same way as his marker all the time. He didn't touch the ball for ages.

Then, disaster! Steelhouse were too confident and they were careless. As they attacked, they left only one defender in place, Porky.

Suddenly, Vernon Park played the ball quickly downfield. Porky tripped and a nippy little striker ran on all alone to score easily.

Vernon Park exploded with joy.

Steelhouse had red faces all round, especially Senna the goalie. He had only let five in all season.

A couple of Steelhouse players glared at Del as if it was his fault they were losing.

'Come on, Del. Do something!' snapped Cropper their big defender. 'We're normally three-up by now!'

'COME ON!' Now Harry Green was leaping up and down. 'For heaven's sake, Del! Get on with it!'

Then the chance came. Del captured a careless pass from the Vernon sweeper. Their keeper was out on the edge of the box. Their goal gaped like the Channel Tunnel.

'Hit it!' yelled Cropper.

'Hit it!' screamed Cyrus.

'Have a go, Del!' squeaked Spanner.

'For goodness sake, hit it!!' ranted Harry Green almost chewing the turf.

But Del didn't hit it, he put his foot on the ball and stood still.

'What's he doing?' Harry Green's glasses had misted over. 'The lad's gone potty!!'

The Vernon keeper took advantage of the miracle to run like mad towards his goal.

The big Vernon sweeper who had made the mistake ran at Del. But – *flick* – with one neat kick Del lifted the ball over the boy's head and ran past him.

Then the keeper charged out. *Flick* – and the ball flew over his head.

Del ran round the back of him, caught the ball on his right foot and rolled it gently into the open goal.

The whole place burst out clapping and cheering. Even some of the Vernon Park lads joined in. It was football magic – the way they play in Brazil. But this was only Stockdale and Del Taylor.

'A genius!' shouted Harry Green. 'What did I tell you? A genius.'

Del walked back to the centre spot, cool as ice.

Now leave me alone, he thought.

He looked up seriously at his dad and raised a hand slightly. Their eyes met. His dad looked puzzled.

29

CHAPTER 4

Penalty!

Half-time was full of excitement. Vernon Park looked worried. Steelhouse were buzzing, eyes shining. It was still 1–1, but they were on their way. They had Del!

Del sat quietly as usual. His mind was made up.

'Take them apart, Del!' said big Cropper. 'We can put six past them this time.'

Spanner just patted him on the arm with stars in his eyes.

The second half started with Del playing back in defence.

'Get up there, Del!' Harry was screaming and waving him forward to the attack.

Del looked up and saw his dad's face high up above the scoreboard. He thought Dad too might go mad, waving him upfield. But no, his dad was standing with his hand on his chin, looking thoughtful.

Del drifted back and back and back. This meant that Del was there to stop Vernon Park scoring. But Steelhouse didn't score either.

There was less than ten minutes left of the game. Something had to happen. Then a Vernon defender kicked a high ball downfield. The ball skidded off a Steelhouse knee.

Corner!

'Back, lads!' yelled Harry. 'Five minutes left! Get ready for the corner.'

Del jogged into position and glanced up again. No Dad!

The kick was taken just as Del's dad walked into the arena. The ball fizzed hard and low across the goal mouth.

It clipped someone's heel and flicked up on to Del's hand.

'PENALTY!!!!!!!'

The ref was pointing at the penalty spot and the place was in uproar.

'You DUCK EGG, DEL!'

Cropper was face to face with him. He looked ready to punch him.

'It hit me – right? I'm not Superman!' said Del as he walked away with his back to everyone.

'Give me strength!!' roared Harry. 'He's blown it for us, now. We're going to lose!'

In went the penalty. 2–1 to Vernon Park.

Five more minutes, thought Del, as he trailed back to the centre. Then it's over. No more football for me.

Then he heard his dad's voice.

'DEL!'

He glanced across. He saw the sad look in his dad's eye and walked across to be shouted at, as usual.

Up at the bar window, City players were grinning and pulling faces. Del thought he heard someone laugh, 'Wonder-boy! Wonder-boy!'

Why couldn't they just let him be? Why couldn't they leave him to enjoy his football instead of expecting him to be some kind of goal machine?

On the Vernon Park bench everyone was laughing too. His dad looked terrible.

'Dad?'

'Don't worry, son. I saw what happened...' Then he patted Del on the shoulder. 'Never mind... it wasn't your fault. Show them what you can do!' He gave his City team mates a nasty look as he jerked a thumb towards them.

As Del walked back to the middle, the eyes of all his mates arrowed into him.
He could almost feel their angry thoughts.

This was why he wasn't going to play again. Ever.

Then, as he came up to the centre circle, Spanner ran over to him. Poor Spanner! There'd be no winner's medal for him today after all. But he wasn't angry with Del.

'It wasn't your fault, Del!' he said loyally. 'You'll show them, won't you? Look, their keeper's off his line again!'

Del took a crafty look. Spanner was right.

The Vernon keeper had run out cheering when they scored the penalty. He was still way out, joking with a defender – the idiot!

Now, with three minutes remaining, there was no time for circus tricks like before.

The jeers of the City team swirled round in Del's head. Suddenly, he was angry. Yes, he'd show them.

'Touch it to me, Span!' he said.

Spanner kicked off. Del took the ball and he was away. Five steps inside the Vernon half, he smashed the ball over the keeper's head...

...and into the back of the net. 2–2.

The teams kicked off again. And, before the Vernon team had finished arguing, Spanner sent Del his first straight pass of the evening. With the ball under perfect control, Del swerved left, and then right, past four defenders.

Then he fooled the goal keeper into diving the wrong way and ran neatly past him.

Del could easily have put the ball into the open net. But he didn't, he stopped.

The defenders all ran at him, desperately. Spanner was charging up alone on the other side like a mad horse. Del carefully sidefooted the ball right across the face of the goal.

Even Spanner could not miss from less than a metre out.

The stadium exploded with yells of disbelief. Spanner disappeared under the excited Steelhouse team as he bounded round the pitch waving his arms and shouting.

YEHHAHHHHH!!!!

The last minute crawled round as Del took the ball and kept it under his control until the whistle went. 3–2 to Steelhouse!

The whole Steelhouse team went mad, cheering and shouting. That is – all except Del. He stood in the centre circle, his heart thundering with excitement.

This is special, he thought. I'll always remember today! And Spanner, who hadn't turned on him after that penalty. Even though he wanted his medal more than anything. Spanner was a real friend.

But he also remembered the jeerers in the City team who were now cheering their heads off. For a whole minute he stared and stared at them, stony-faced.

Then he joined the Steelhouse lads on their lap of honour. Everyone wanted to praise him. Could he turn his back on this? But this was only when you won, wasn't it?

Cropper came up, head bowed. 'Sorry about yelling at you, Del. I was out of order,' he said. 'You were fantastic!'

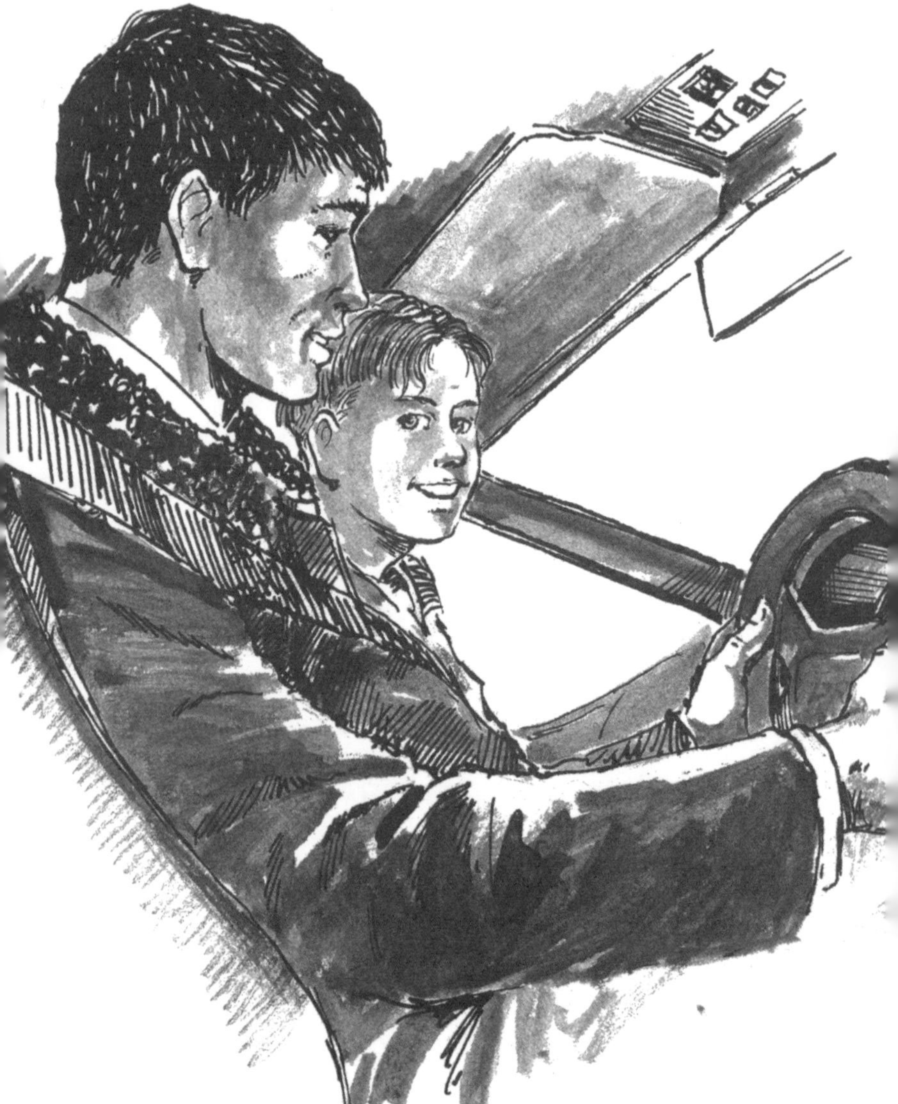

CHAPTER 5

The winner

Soon everyone had their medals and Del was on his way home. His dad was glowing with pride.

'Brilliant, just brilliant,' he said. 'You gave it to Spanner on purpose, didn't you? You set it up because he's your friend! He's the worst player on the team, isn't he?'

Del just laughed.

'He scored though, didn't he?'

Good old Spanner!

'Okay?' said his mum when they arrived back.

'Fantastic!' said his dad. 'He's better than I ever was!'

'What do you want for supper, Del?' asked his mum. 'Something special for a winner?'

'No, Mum, I'm tired. I'll just have a cup of tea.'

And off he went to his room to flop on his bed. On went his Walkman. The booming music might stop the thoughts whizzing about in his head. But it was no good. He felt so restless that he couldn't stand up or sit down and feel comfortable.

He thought he heard a creak on the stairs, but decided it was nothing. Then he stood staring at his wall of souvenirs and photographs. Time to go to bed maybe?

He tried to take his tracksuit top off without removing the medal from round his neck. The ribbon snapped and the gold prize spun on to the floor.

But he didn't pick it up. He peeled off his shirt, walked towards the window, walked back then stopped in front of the fallen medal.

At that moment, his dad walked in with a cup of tea, picked up the medal and handed it and the tea to Del with a sad smile.

'Plenty more to come, eh?'

Del said nothing. I'm never going to be able to tell him, he thought. His dad sat next to him on the bed.

'Funny thing, people,' started his dad. 'Like those lads back at the club. Thought I knew them...'

What's he talking about? thought Del. What's he getting at?

'What are you trying to tell me, Dad?'

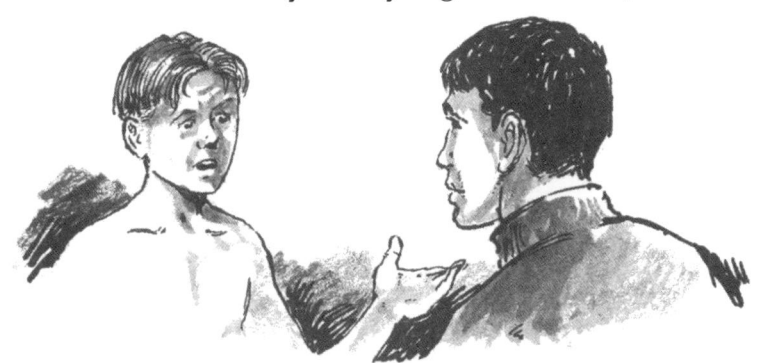

' '... Then I realized, tonight. How much they rate people just because they're winners.' His dad hesitated.

'Well, football's been my whole life and football up there is about winning, just winning. But I saw your face after that penalty... heard those jeering idiots in the bar... Then I saw your medal on the floor just now and I realized that I'm no better than them.'

'No, Dad! There are always people like that at matches, I'm used to it...' Del started.

'Thanks, son, but you're wrong to make excuses for me. I'm not "people", I'm your DAD, Del! I want you to do... what you like doing... If you choose to do something else... well... it's all right by me, okay?'

He patted Del on the shoulder and he stood up without looking the boy in the eye. It had been hard to say it, Del knew.

The big, strong footballer started towards the door.

Del's voice stopped him.
'Thanks, Dad!'
His dad turned and without another word went downstairs.

For a second, Del felt a ton lighter.

I don't have to play any more! he thought. I'm free!

But then he felt empty. He remembered the lovely feeling as the ball flies off your foot into the net. And then there was everyone else on the team.

He walked across his room to the shield on the wall and draped the medal over it with all the others. When he was over there the Steelhouse team photo caught his eye.

He imagined the glowing faces of the lads tonight. Cropper, Porky, Senna, Cyrus and especially Spanner, would be at home now, waving their medals about, telling their mums and dads all about it.

Then ringing their uncles and aunties and friends to repeat it all over again.

But the one that stood out was Spanner, tall and blond and lanky, left-footed and played down the right! Useless, but mad keen... only on the team because his mum ran a launderette. And now he was a hero! Because of Del.

After the presentation, Spanner had come up to Del with tears in his eyes and given him a big hug.

'Del,' he said, 'this is the best day of my whole life...' and then his voice had faded away.

Del stared hard at the picture – at Spanner's bony chest puffed out in pride and the horrible wire glasses that he'd forgotten to take off for the team photo.

Okay, Spanner, you win! he thought.

He smiled, scratched his head, put his boots and trainers under his bed, walked to the door and called downstairs.

'Hey, Dad, who are we playing on Saturday?'

About the author

I have been involved in football all my life, playing in the streets and parks of Stockport when I was younger. The person who owned the ball would always choose whether to play striker or goalie!

Later, I watched Stockport County and Manchester City, and played as a 'sweeper' for several amateur teams. I was not quite skilful enough to be a professional. But I did coach school teams as a teacher and still love the game and all the Spanners who still play in it.